salmonpoetry

Diverse Voices from Ireland and the World

Zen Traffic Lights (Lapwing, 2005)

A Father's Day (Salmon, 2008)

Session (Salmon, 2011)

How to Bake a Planet (Salmon, 2016)

We are
the Walrus

Poems by

PETE MULLINEAUX

Published in 2022 by
Salmon Poetry
Cliffs of Moher, County Clare, Ireland
Website: www.salmonpoetry.com
Email: info@salmonpoetry.com

ISBN 978-1-915022-23-3

Cover photograph: *mikeuk – istockphoto.com*
Walrus drawing on title page: *Kathleen Furey*
Cover Design & Typesetting: *Siobhán Hutson*

Printed in Ireland by Sprint Print

Salmon Poetry gratefully acknowledges the support of
The Arts Council / An Chomhairle Ealaíon

For all creatures, great and small

CONTENTS

Nature and Us

Us and our nature

Musical Break

Coda

Nature and Us

A pangolin goes into a bar

climbs up onto a high stool, orders a drink —
ant-termite cocktail in an extra-tall glass,

turns down a straw, accepts a slice of lemon,
wistful reminder of the moon peeking through

treetops, or hanging above a burnt-out savannah…
'Haven't seen you out this way before,' says the

barman, 'you must've travelled some distance'.
'Yes, quite a journey,' replies the stranger, 'the

traffic was crazy, lucky to be still in one piece.'
'Well, aren't we all globetrotters, I guess you're

related to those Armadillos?' The pangolin yawns,
glances around, 'I like the relaxed ambience here,

any chance of a room? I need a place to lie low.'
A frown as the guest book is offered: 'Did I hear

something about a small spot of bother out East?'
The head nods, 'The victim often gets the blame;

now the bats are feeling the heat. Myself, I like to
steer clear of trouble, out on the wide open plain

or hidden deep in dappled solitude of shadows,
somnambulant drip-drip of raindrops on leaves…'

'Well you'll be in your element here, the weather
we're getting — global warming! But don't they say

the cure is in the pain? And no harm in keeping
your powder dry, but once you've had a little nap

I'm betting that long tongue will be glad to loosen up, you'll be fond of the old *scéal* like anyone else.'

'I suppose we all have our strange stories to tell,' says the visitor, licking its lips.

Summer Time

When the living is neither easy nor straightforward;
Yesterday shows a puzzled face – overnight a sleight
of hands has edged us along; we've bought ourselves
Time, so we can have later sunsets, even as body clocks
resist the retreat from morning light.

Do we need a little darkness?

Spinning the wheel further ahead to our day of reckoning –
dire forecasts confirmed: ice gone, sea lapping at throats…
looking back and asking, did we gain or lose that hour?

Verified

My computer tells me it's cloudy, raining,
I look out the window...and gosh, so it is...

We are the Walrus

Harbinger or in search of safe harbour –
a young pup fetches up on our shores
thousands of miles from its Arctic home;
straight out of a *selkie* tale, enchanting
us with its whiskers and two-pronged
smile, shimmering blubber; for a while it
takes centre stage and being a rock star
with a voice like a siren, draws crowds...

Then onto an outgoing wave, following
the current or its nose, heading for the
next gig: the Welsh coast, after that it's
southern France, then Spain – the return
flipper via Iceland, arriving hopefully in
its natural place, joining fellow walruses
chilling in the surf, high on salty sea-weed,
exchanging their own fabulous stories of
love and loss, foreboding – perhaps one
about a human child in a seal-like skin,
its world swept off-course – searching
the rocks for pattern and meaning in
heaps of tusks, untouched oysters ...

Covid Conversation

I'm out in the garden, replenishing the feeder
listening to the birds, their songs and chatter...

do they sense something different in the air –
is this peanuts compared to their own losses?

Long-eared

Coming in at dusk from checking the clothesline
I hear flapping, and for a moment think it must be
some bath towels left out to dry overnight – when
something flies over my head – our owls are back!
They migrate here each year from across the lake,
once it gets cold enough on this side, or so I'm told.
     Huge, it glides away between the pine and
monkey-puzzle. Usually there are two; last year we
heard the distinctive call of a chick, then one evening,
three in the air at once!
     Such a privilege to be here: the sky, the stars,
     these swooping shadows...

Now it's four in the morning and I can't sleep –
heartbeat, breath – wind in the trees; on quieter
nights I hear their wheezing as dawn approaches,
a sound they make before setting off to hunt –
building like an engine...

How to build a rook's nest

Pick a tall tree to make a strong mast.
      The first stick must be suspended
in such a way, say, between two fingers
      of a fork in a branch, so not to fall
when a second is laid delicately across…
      then the beak slips a third in-between –
a game of spillikins in reverse…

Again and again, until there it is:
      not for this dark rogue the robin's
symmetrical bowl of twigs, grass
      moss and leaves, softened with fine
hair or feathers –
      altogether a madder looking
assemblage, but one that will still
      hold the treasured eggs, let
these pirates of the high rigging
      whistle and crow like any
deck-hugging songbird.

Earthstars

Geastrum triplex

Shooting from below
    out of the dark matter
    that forms the underworld web
their fungi ancestors arrived here
even before plants, yet, somehow
    ended up closer to ourselves
    breathing the same oxygen
        suffering bacterial infections
    though even as they decay
        microscopic threads spread
            new life to their loam-home...

Stars of wonder, stars of darkness!
feeling our dull tread on their ceiling
        how they must pity
            these poor relations
      stumbling above them
        blinded by light

Boarders

A scuffling in the bushes,
I soften my breathing and wait...
until a perfect *broc* face peeks
out of the inky dark – a second
rough shape untangles itself
from a pile of hedge trimmings,
a matted hairbrush.
      Some busy nosing
before both melt back
into the shadows...

I feel honoured, does this mean
they'll be staying: cousins to
otter, mink, pine martin, wolverine!
I've heard they trample flowers,
will make a golf course of the lawn
rooting for grubs. Perhaps if I learn
their language we can set up a dialogue,
find a compromise over right of way,
borders – discover some natural
accommodation.

Who knows, with all that digging
those squat snouts may yet
unearth a poem.

Lamb/s

Jaunty gymnasts
on their grass
trampoline

woolly jumpers
suspended
in a green sky

World doing
a somersault
turning life

on its head…
perceptions
out of joint.

Bovine Heaven

In the living fields,
three cow generations: calf
mother, grandmother.

In Praise of Idleness

A bullfinch is perched
on the edge
of a flower pot

pecking seeds
from a
dandelion…

I could watch
all day –
one, two, three o'clock…

Horses

Three of them out on the road,
the gate into their field
swinging open...

full of frisk, but nervous too
in this freedom
and so they should be, near

as they are to a blind bend...
I call to them, try to get in
behind, but they back away

closer to the danger. The sound
of an engine...I panic, retreat,
hold the gate wider,

hissing, "Please, horses"...
They seem to understand –
nod their beautiful heads,

trotting on through, even
as a lorry arrives, just
in time to see the gap

closing on something
that never happened.

Grandma's Footsteps

Brazen as the sun burning the tarmac
a red fox watches me approach in my
walker's high-vis jacket

as if trying to decide if I'm a tree
or a flower, then gives me the brush off,
skips over a wall into a field

stopping a few times, turning
its head back to see
if I've moved...

Worth it!

She kicks her paws and spurts
along the shoreline

rushes at the waves to
great white suds of applause

emerges from dissolving foam
like a canine Aphrodite

shakes out wet fur, showers
the world with her salt.

Game Pheasant

Turning a bend in the laneway…
a kick to my heart
at the sudden commotion!
It's like we've both heard a shot
as you rise to the safety of a tree
heaving your bulk like an overburdened helicopter.

Another time, in the car, I came upon you
where there was no cover, you ran ahead
       swerving from side to side
a fugitive trying to shake off a pursuer,
distrustful of what should be your natural element;
it's fixed in the DNA: terror sounds of grass-beaters,
rifles bolt-loading, gun-dogs panting.
Funny how a pheasant hunt is called a *drive* –
some smart-alec people post videos
filmed from dash-cams of such *birdbrain* behaviour,
not recognising a hard-gained survival instinct –
will we get even close to your 20 million years?

I hear you sometimes at night –
that anguished call announcing yourself
in the safety of the dark, saying
how you are game but not *game*.
Oh foolish pheasant, oh foolish heart…

Interference

Two caterpillars crossing the road...
I use a leaf to pick them up, just as

a car arrives, is forced to slow — faces
through a wet windscreen look unsure

whether to mock or applaud, perhaps
they'll argue over it later? I carry my

vessel carefully to the verge, continue
walking, mulling over what happened,

this random event, my moment playing
God; might I have disturbed a delicate

balance in our journeys (think butterfly
wings), a couple discovering they aren't

well-suited, caterpillars carrying a sense
of dislocation in how they got from there

to here...

Uplift

A sudden roar of aircraft —
but no chalky lines etching the skies;
it's the high point of the pandemic
and we're grounded, though not yet
fully earthed.

I adjust my senses, realise it's coming
from the hedgerow...there in ivy-wrapped
hawthorn, a swarm of bees, buzzing like crazy
in a rush of nectar, like they've been given
a free holiday.

I think back to those blind musicians —
Raftery, O'Carolan — how it must have been
for them, plodding the old roads, ears tuned
to most sounds, yet pulled-up by a tree
full of passengers taking off...

Us and our nature

Hairdressing

Lockdown – and the locks are down
around my neck. My partner takes up
the comb and scissors, tells me to sit,
observes I'm a little tense, teases –
"relax, unlock".

Without the familiar background buzz
of radio, we chit-chat about this and
that, catching up on world developments,
a phone call from our daughter, a recent
podcast on 'dealing with the void'. I say,
"You have a sensitive touch" – and yes,
not bad, a brand new look...

Later, passing by a neighbouring field –
a horse sidles over for a head rub, mane
tangled with burrs. I carefully unpick,
unwind, discarding each curler,
enquiring how her day has been so far?

Finished, I wonder about that long fringe,
shall we sign off with a parting?

Matryoshka

Like those Russian or Chinese dolls –
the tiny anchovies tin
            squeezes into the slightly
            larger one for sardines –
            then that nests cosily inside
            a lentils can; finally this set
            of three fits neatly into the
            empty shell of a margarine
            tub –

I stand back, pleased with this small effort
towards recycling, waste management – even
as I'm thinking about where it will end up –
some toxic dump – kicking the cans down
the road as it were, not to mention I really
should be eating less tinned foods,
and of course there's the fish…

I was reading too how those dolls have become
a metaphor for offshore shell companies.

I've washed and rinsed away the salty brine
but the fishy smell lingers … thoughts inside
of thoughts, inside of thoughts, and only my
head swimming.

Trust Games

She's gone inside, this time it's win or bust,
beyond simply another routine test;
I wait in the car, tell myself to trust.

A Jag charges into the next bay, kicking up dust,
the driver leaves his radio babbling – pest!
She's gone inside, this time it's win or bust.

I receive a text: *delay...consultant late...must*
be held up. My neighbour yawns, takes a rest
as I wait in the car and tell myself to trust

in guardian angels, that all will be well, lust
for some reassurance the hospital's guest
is in safe hands; that she'll win, they'll bust

a gut to make it so; afterwards she'll be fussed
over as they offer tea. Ah, who'd have guessed:
as I wait in the car and will myself to trust

he finally emerges from his vehicle, a gust
of wind blows a plastic nametag east to west.
He puts on his mask. She's waiting inside....

We're in it together

Spider Man's inky shadow, Sherlock's Moriarty:
inner and outer demons to be mind-wrestled. Try
to run and I'm dark energy, dragging your soles
in nightmare mud; nemesis of self-doubt, vortex
sucking you down, a voice saying: *'No escape,
travel to the edges, I'll still be here...'*

We are like Siamese twins wrongly separated –
inevitably you'll have to face me; but no need
for a face-off, once you accept I'm merely part
of your alter-ego, mirror to your thoughts. Let
me travel the road with you, move in the same
direction, like a tandem bicycle. We can share
the work: freewheel a while – lift those furious
feet off the pedals...

Dissenter

for Zhang Zhan

Discord is as necessary as concord –
music history a pendulum's swing
between harmony and dissonance;
in Hegel's philosophy, no thesis to
synthesis without antithesis. Marcuse
said all transcendent art has to destroy
complacency, superficial consensus.

"At the risk of striking an off-note," she
says before each grand assembly of those
who espouse certainty; to whom she is
agitator and whistleblower, a girl who
won't stay mum – sitting alone on some
stone steps, making her small voice heard –
with her many names: Cassandra, Antigone,
Joan, Rosa, Malala, Greta…

With Bob On Our Side

(on his 80th birthday)

"Come see this strange guy on TV" –
my mother calling, and there he was,
an outcast angel rattling the gates of
Eden with a guitar and harmonica (oh
the cool neck rack), rebel with a cause.

Biting the apple, everything changed:
through school assemblies, dull lessons
my friends and I mouthed lyrics to one
another, had every line off pat (how our
history teacher would have liked similar
devotion to those dates of battles).

We became attuned to this otherworld
where his heartfelt songs kept time, tales
of love, loss; protest against intolerance,
racial prejudice – cruel deaths of Medgar
Evans, Hattie Carroll; injustice of corrupt
systems: George Jackson, Hurricane Carter.

When I went on demos to support civil rights
in Northern Ireland, linked arms against the
bomb, South African Apartheid, it was good
to know that while many of those lined up with
batons believed God was standing right behind
them, we innocents had Bob on our side.

Men Women and Doors

Growing up in the 1960's, many tradesmen arrived
at our front door – postman, milkman, insurance man,
football pools man; while others delivered around
the back – coalman, paraffin man, or stopped at the
gate – dustman, pig-man taking away our slops in a
bucket. In summer an ice-cream man moored his van
to the kerb, rang its jingle; and for some time we had
the novelty of a driving instructor parking his car
with the big red 'L' sign, pressing the doorbell to pick
up our mum, looking her best...

Mothers welcomed these men, their usefulness,
casual cheer, even if a few of them were grumpy;
each woman offered thanks, closed her door, returned
to the internal world of housework and daydreaming.
A few double-jobbed: Mrs A did needlework, raised
and lowered hems on skirts, shortened and extended
shirt cuffs and trouser bottoms; Mrs B cut and styled
the hair of young and old; both experts in adjustment.
They minded one another's children, often feeding a
small tribe. Occasionally they entertained, gave out
treats, or finger-wagged at mischief – others provided
glamour, glitzy fashions, new lines in makeup.

Sometimes these indoor-women went out, usually to the
shops, or to bring the children home from school. Then in
the evening, they'd be home, awaiting spouses bringing
their outdoors lives with them, or leaving it all behind:
these were a mix of talkers and listeners, some moody,
wanting only peace and quiet so wives had to tiptoe
around, careful not to annoy.

After the wheel, perhaps there was no more defining human
invention than the hinged-door – this thing that worked both
ways, allowing the world in or you out. Some houses were
known for their open doors, while others stayed closed with
rumours about what went on behind them – what happened
when inner met outer, warm air greeted cold.

Distancing

P --o
-----------------e --------------------------------------
--------------------------------------m

Swimming with Plato

This is absolutely true – for my first swimming lesson
I went with my mother to a big house in a different part
of the city, climbed several flights of dark stairs, me
wondering, where's the pool? Maybe the posh lady
opening the door to her apartment liked to high dive –
was looking for a young prodigy to teach, like a character
from my sister's *Bunty* comic; or might there be a
descending slide like the one at the public marina?

What the elderly woman (now I could see her in the light)
did have was a table, across which I was asked to lie while
she took my hands, then my feet and showed me the frog
movements of the breaststroke. We didn't attempt the crawl
and I only went one time (my mother had seen the ad
in the paper, gone on a whim) and, as the man said,
it's the thought that counts.

Later on I learnt to swim in the sea like everyone
else; but looking back I realise, despite her limitations,
the old woman had whetted my appetite, as well as
opening my mind to how a kitchen table can become
a pool, a flight of stairs might lead to the high board;
how so often we find ourselves making do.

Wrench

The distant voice on the line suggests
I go find one...then it's simply a matter
of locating the external stopcock. Water

is now streaming out from the leak and
I'm trying to shut off reverberations
from that gut-tightening word, wishing

I had the contact for that other plumber
who came so quickly the last time the
pipes froze, who arrived as they say

at the drop of a hat (or a drop of water!)
remembering too how the three of us
drank a few beers afterwards to celebrate...

and now that I've somehow managed
to stem the outflow, wrung out all the
handkerchiefs, put a stopper on this

sodden episode, thinking more clearly...
I realize of course it had to be you
that took the number down.

Duelling with Descartes

Hoisted on my father's shoulders, borrowing his bulk for a better view
of the parade, I'm a mahout aboard an elephant. And now I'm that
goddess adorning the prow of a boat, until the next float arrives and I
become the tiny capsule atop a giant Saturn rocket…

> A fiery flare, we separate – like a ladder has been kicked away
> I'm pedalling air, rising into the stratosphere, pure thought…
> Here comes the moon! I orbit three times, glimpse its dark side
> wonder about life down there. Where next – Pluto?
> Or further, beyond the pull of gravity…

But the blue Earth beckons; descent begins. To avoid a hard landing, I
plunge into the ocean, causing giant waves or rather a few
modest ripples as I sink slowly into the bath water, achieve
near-horizontal, mind and body for once a level playing field,
view my torso, or is it my father's? Stretched out, detached
an uncharted island waiting to be inhabited.
I watch as my feet lift themselves
one at a time, toes pressing against
both cold and hot taps…

Feeling our way in Friesland

The sat-nav voice tells our driver when we need to turn,
but otherwise stays mute. At complex intersections the
interjections become more like chatter, almost a fellow-
passenger – the speaker is Dutch so we can only sit back
and enjoy the word-music, its rise and fall, ebb and flow.

A walking tour of Harlingen's canals and seaboard
reveals areas of higher ground, *'terps'* – artificial mounds
made by the townspeople for precious sanctuary at times
of flooding. 'These are our mountains' the guide jokes.
Later, we walk the braille-ridge of an ancient dyke.

The journey's neither straight nor flat, our minds trace
a raised border containing the land, fingertips and soles
mapping the proud interior as islands of letters link up
like stepping stones to form names of towns – Pingjum

Makkum, Workum, Dokkum: communality of expression
in word endings – heartfelt definitions of belonging, each
place-name a raft of tenuous buoyancy above the rising
waterline, babble and erosion of encroaching seas.

Poetry Visit

They're 11 years old and learning how to write poetry –
playing with words that describe moving water: 'flow',
'gush', 'splash!' Then for contrast, a city scene: I ask
them to imagine a giant crane, wrecking-ball swinging
on a chain, demolishing buildings – a row of houses, a
whole neighbourhood. They call out 'smash!' 'bang!'
'rubble'. One quiet kid waits for calm, then whispers
'Adam's apple...'

A few groans; some stare, others look away. I'm lost
for words too, a lump in my throat...

The Cure at Oran's Well

for the O'Toole Brothers, Galway

The car is a little under the weather – definitely giving
a bumpier ride. I leave it in the garage, and to kill time
take a stroll down Oran's hill towards the sacred well.

A ring of stone wall, with an iron gate acting as a clasp
suggesting a piece of natural jewellery; shiny emerald
leaves of hart's tongue fern have colonised the space,

even the hole itself, almost dry, to which I'm drawn,
descending four ancient steps to peer beneath the stone
lintel into a dark cavity the shape of a tomb, yet offering

life's elixir. I ask for an ending to the siege laying waste
our world. My own modest repairs will take a couple
of hours and I've brought along a book – Ruth Padel's

The Poem and the Journey – enjoy the way she strips poems
down, reassembles them so lovingly – I smile at the thought
my car might be experiencing the same attentive treatment.

And then the gift of a real-life drama, as a truck reverses
down the *boreen* and two women enter a nearby field –
returning with each holding the bridle of a horse; one

distrusting foal refuses, and they have to coax it in with
soft words and treats: horse power! They make several
trips until their task is completed and I stand, applaud.

Mind and soul satiated, I re-climb the hill to find Martin
O'Toole emerging from beneath a VW camper like Odran
of Iona rising from the dead. His brother Peter, more akin to

the local saint, passes me my keys, clutching a torn rag in
his other hand – and suddenly I see them hanging from every
aerial and wing mirror! He mentions something about the

suspension: protective bushings, springs, but all cured!
I present my card for payment, wishing I could give
thanks another way – throw a clutch of bright coins

into his palm, even better, some form of water container –
a sump or tub, the open cap of that blown radiator leaning
against a wall, let them drop

one by one, adding a prayer with each small *splish* –
for my car facing its upcoming NCT; for all who heal –
mechanics, poets, horses.

Irish Election – All Party Debate

I'm watching it on TV, rooting for the left. But how to unite
red and green? I think back to those once separated Luas lines,

two sets of track, having avoided one another, awaiting final
linkage; earlier, how we'd felt under attack, railed against the

slow labour of inch by inch, flinched at grating metal, blocks
splintering as kerbs and pathways re-aligned like changes in a

language. I remember escaping into a city-centre bookshop
for solitude and a different mode of transportation, a carriage

of the mind; leafing through some pages on 1916 (when trams
were the future!), recalling too those dual-colour glasses worn

once upon a time at 3-D movies, green and red merging to form
a single vision – and perhaps we'll yet see a way of joining up

the dots, providing natural flow from green to red, red to green:
clinking of coupling as Merrion Square, the scenic expanse of

Phoenix Park, links arms with Tallaght, Crumlin, Finglas…

The Screen

(after Edvard Munch)

During the night my brain switches on like a computer booting itself up, and here are all the files that contain my life! I try counting documents to get back to sleep, but that makes me toss and turn even more. I delete a few but suspect I'll be up in the morning rooting through the bin.

I give myself over to pondering some outstanding work/relationship issues — wonder is it possible to solve by simply cutting and pasting from one file to another? It seems to work: yes, save!

I surf a while until I'm almost drifting off, when there's an incoming email — see it's a person I'd rather avoid, put up my firewall, bar the doorway into my mind, but then worry that somewhere in my head's chat rooms, I might have left a window open...

Possibly a Poem about Patriarchy

This came from a dream…
we fathers have arrived to pick up our kids
from playschool…
     to find the building on fire, flames raging — we're told
not to enter, the burning roof is about to collapse —
     but each man hears an inner voice commanding, "Save your child!"
and so we all dash in, search frantically around, desperately calling out
names, but with falling timbers, the smoke and the confusion of bodies
crashing into one another, it's seemingly hopeless, until
     a different voice speaks to all at once: "You have just a few precious
seconds; rescue one child, *any* child"… so each grabs the nearest one
                   and escapes

     not a moment
          or another thousand years
        to spare…

Closing the Gap

An official form requires my mother's maiden name:
Prosser, Welsh — the spiral movement of the pen
spins me back to the northern outskirts of Bristol,
our family piling into an ancient Vauxhall for a day
trip across the Severn via the old Aust-Beachley
Ferry, muddied surface waves rippling
over hidden depths...

As I sign my name, the word-strewn page
looks akin to overgrowth on a disused road or
railway line — an ancient track beside the Wye —
all that is hidden from history, forgotten routes
winding back to the lands of our mothers.

Falling for Fruit

Afterwards, he told me I'd eaten six. I hadn't actually been
counting, somewhat scattered by the gloomy surroundings
and how quickly events were unfolding. Besides, it was quite
a journey down, I hadn't had lunch, I was starving. A few, a
handful, does it matter when apparently even one would have
sufficed, served to do the trick? When it comes to handing over
control the rules are rarely made clear. Naturally, neither I nor
my stricken mother had any say; no-one of my gender in fact.
This well-worn story has many variations in the telling: initial
abduction, all that happened next; the clinching evidence
usually the same – I took them voluntarily.

The truth is the earth opened up as he took me by force from my
walk in the sun; I didn't know him, but seemingly he knew me.
Please, let's debunk all this pretence I grew fond of him, that he
wasn't such a bad old fucker, once you got to know him, that my
mother had to fight with both of us, before dragging me back up
towards the light. Pomegranate seeds: did you ever? How did the
trial go: "She was wandering alone in bare feet, sandals dangling
seductively by their straps from her curled ring-less third finger –
bare legs your Honour!" Brother Zeus concurred. Pomegranates,
figs, apples – what's this weird thing these gods have with fruit:
cue women's fall from grace. We discover gravity early on, it's
in the basic training – men must wait 'till it hits them on the head.

Disturbed

It enters my head like tinnitus at full volume; I see it
     hovering
a sci-fi bird of prey. Once on a nature programme
they played the call of a Red Kite, but this isn't a living
thing – nor is it a kite, no string leads back to a controlling
hand.

A moment ago the scene was in animated conversation
with itself – seagulls, children, thump of a football,
roar of surf, back-suck of retreating waves over shingle,
     'buzzoom' from a darting bee…
       but this sterile drone
enforces a strict monotone, drowning out
     everything else. I look for fellow sufferers, potential objectors –
     some gaze up, curious, bemused; others appear oblivious.
So I try disengagement, blending the noise into the general
     ambience; resist an urge to stick fingers in both ears,
     mute that inner voice insisting any second
       claws might open –
          a bomb
          drop

More!

(The opening song from *Oliver* updated and aligned to the law of diminishing returns)

Chickin wing, onion ring, curry sauce on everything
chip, dip, egg flip – pumpkin seed and apple pip
meat, sweet, sugar-beet – can you hear the sugar beat
in the beat box, cereal box, booze on rocks in the ice box
ice box, iced tea, wake on up and smell the coffee!
Fish soup, spaghetti hoop, watermelon, cantaloupe
Sunday roast, cheese on toast – feeding hunger, coast to coast
deep fry, shepherd's pie, reach up for that pie in the sky!
Chocolate muffin, turkey stuffin', shovel it down can't get enough in
fill the space, fill the gap – fill the void when life feels crap
more and more – wondering why and what it's for
feed the rich, starve the poor – some get less, some get more
feed the rich, starve the poor – then go off and start a war
cus those at the top want more and more
who knows what the hell it's for
just keep grabbing more and more
more and more
more and more
more and more....

Another Toy Story

Long before I'd read *Bury my Heart at Wounded Knee,*
Black Elk Speaks – knew about the Choctaw's 'trail of tears',
I was eight years old – innocent and ignorant, playing
Cowboys & Indians with the other kids, shouting
"Geronimo" as we jumped from ledges and trees.

At some point my parents gave me a present of a real
set of bow and arrows, bought from a shop, along with
a bull's-eye target to shoot at (to save our back door!).
I improvised a quiver and saved up my pocket money
to buy more arrows, loving the varied colours of the
flight feathers. And there I was, Chingachgook
in my own dark woods.

I still have them: my oldest possessions, along with one
Hornby train engine, a lone survivor from what was
once a railway set...and now, looking to pass these
things on, I'm caught by the irony of bow and arrows
alongside a steam train – the Iron Horse: how these
not so innocent toys speak to one another...

The World Shrugs

This image might suggest
a stunted Mexican wave, still sluggishly circulating,
a dying-swan dance for shoulders, shaking
off burdens of expectation, of having to be excited,
each pair saying: 'Why look at me?' or 'So what,
c'est la vie, it's the way of the world.'

As if like Atlas, we'd be left with the weight of the world
forever; yet that initial elevation suggests
something stirring, each mind asking, 'What
part can I play?' There's blood circulating,
muscles being activated, becoming excited,
the body, like a cocktail tumbler shaking...

But then – the pitiful slump (sky falling), shaking
of the head to confirm a negative: 'Sorry world
you're on your own.' Instead, get super-excited
over humdrum decisions, a ruse that suggests
you're on top of everything, circulating
at least in the right orbits, forget what

might have been a higher calling; strike 'what
if...' from the agenda, allow nothing earthshaking
as you join the choral indifference circulating
like a carousel ride: up, down...a carefree world
even if that grip on the horse's pole suggests
fear of falling, getting too excited.

The future then: an alien Darwin lands, excited
to find a fossilised corpse, caught mid-gesture; asks, what
can this signify? These hunched shoulders suggest
a strong spine, an upright stance...and yet, a shaking
of the head as a Being from another world
can't picture something beyond its own circulating.

It mimics the upturned palms, another signal circulating
amongst these creatures: *Hope, helplessness?* Excited
yet saddened, our scientist conjures a brave world
in the making, dearly wants to know what
might have befallen it, what planet-shaking
extinction event would these clues suggest?

Excited, if muted, the thought now circulating
suggests a world ending not with a bang, even a whimper,
a shaking-off of something...but what?

A Future Nature Lover Reflects

At last the woods are full of life again —
creepy-crawly things, other delights
on the wing. A regular beat: no rain
or flood, burning sun or sombre Arctic
mood will mean the failure of a brood —
no threat of a permanent silence, all is
improved, more resilient, you can set
your time by swallows coming and
going, a cuckoo's call.

Sad perhaps to think of what was lost
but now and then, no harm in overhaul.
Artificial? Let us say rather: 'artifice'.
Today, nothing needs to feel the cold,
thrushes sing in the astro-snow, a newly
sprung robin finds its perch with a steely
'ping', sings its hopes, this joyful world
embracing. A flash of jay! All of nature
present, everything moving to and fro —
until, in the far-off future, systems slow...
long-life batteries will need replacing.

'Don't always expect fireworks...'

is my opening line at the poetry workshop I'm about to facilitate,
'...or feel you have to say something profound, or entertain: just

observe what is going on, both inside and out, then try to capture
some of that in your choice of words.' One man says he finds

the whole thing terrifying: he used to sea-fish – hurricanes, sharks,
don't come near the sinking feeling when facing a blank page... (I'm

off on my own fantasy here: the shipwrecked sailor, miles of blinding
white sand, a cruel sun judging from above...) Someone asks me to

explain metaphors; another frowning face wants to know, 'What's
wrong with expecting fireworks?' I go with this, ask what kind

of firework each would choose if their poem was a self-portrait –
might it be a slow burning Roman Candle, suddenly exploding into life

near the end? 'Mine would most likely fizzle out,' says one woman, wry.
'Because damp got in the box?' a second voice suggests.

'What else could you be: perhaps a rocket – off to a flying start –
an arc of spectacular wordplay, then a dying fall...' 'Sounds like my

other half,' says the group's joker. 'Well...in that case how about a
Jumping Jack? Even make it a concrete poem – text literally hopping

about, or...a Catherine Wheel, spinning crazily on a pin – threatening
to fly off any moment on some dangerous tangent...' There's a groan:

'That's how my *head* feels right now! Can't we just write something?'
'OK,' I say, 'forget about the instructions, reach into the box, select

at random, light the blue touch-paper, stand back at a safe distance;
be prepared for a stuttering start, a sputtering szzzzzzz (?????) but

then, who knows...! – ! – !!!
And of course, be sure to sign your name at the end with a sparkler.

X

Throw it, plant it, exchange it –
a quick peck, or a smacker
lips are essential, tongues optional,
mouth to mouth the general rule, although
cheeks will do –
from a distance you can blow it;
sometimes, during it, you might sigh—
releasing endorphins, oxytocin, dopamine,
serotonin, adrenaline; wet or dry,
always good for saying goodbye,
sealing a promise,
a mark of tenderness on the forehead;
other times it's just for show – kiss-kiss
or once a year under the mistletoe…
best slow…
a few you'll never forget;
Rodin sculpted, Klimt painted
but enough of this,
the pucker muscle
is orbicularis oris,
rhymes with bliss…
x

Musical Break

Ghost Session

(lockdown 2020)

The instruments are there without us, getting ready —
cases open, bellows ease, strings tune — rosin spreads;
some chit-chat about weather, the match, a bit of world
news thrown in. Flute enters, shrugging off the raingear,
bicycle clips; Banjo tries to order drinks, plink-plink of
a coin on an empty glass. A few are already warming to
fingers, loosened wrists, softened lips; taking off into a
genteel O'Carolan set, maybe a jig or two, before letting
rip with some high tempo reels…

Each takes a turn starting: Whistle leans towards polkas
and slides, Fiddle picks a mazurka; they allow a pause
every now and then for *Singer*. The evening repeats more
habits and rituals: Bouzouki will check the soccer scores,
while Mandolin slips out for a smoke; Bodhran is bound
to come back from the loo saying, 'We don't sound so bad
from in there.' Concertina's quiet tonight, maintaining a
distance, squeezing thoughts…

The music fills the absence, names of tunes taking on new
resonance: *Last Night's Fun, Happy to Meet Sorry to Part,
— My Love is in America —* there's a call for "*Ciúnas*" as a
lament is announced, but with no stag parties, darts crowd
to compete with, the TV off, there's already silence…

Magic Fiddle

My teacher plays through the tune
so I can hear how it should sound —
I say "not fair" because it's clearly
a magic fiddle: she must have met
the fairies coming home one night
from a session and traded something
as is the custom. She winks and says
it's true this is a nice instrument, but
the voice whispering in the leaves of
a lone hawthorn spoke about patience,
warned about the many nights lying
awake wondering if this was what
she'd bargained for; but to keep
practising and the magic *inside*
would eventually uproot itself.

She taps her bow three times on the
music stand; we set off slowly,
going around and around until my
eyes close, the jig rhythm enters my
body, the notes trip off my fingers
and it feels like magic as two fiddles
sound like one.

Thinking inside the box

"Everything seemed to be music to him..."

The coastal inlet fills with water, then forces it out –
on each inhale-exhale, a clump of seaweed bunches
then spreads its straggled fronds, a flurry of liquid

notes settling into a knuckled chord. Suck and blow –
I'm thinking of Mairtin O'Connor's button accordion,
how it was heard said he'd likely find the pattern of

music in anything – such as here in this rock pool –
a slow air, even the lilt of a hornpipe, jig or reel
in the repeating stretch and ease, ebb and flow...

*

Like music, language is a living thing, expanding
contracting, sometimes we take short-cuts to speed
matters up: 'button accordion' collapses into 'box',
the more formal name squeezed from the narrative.

A case of false modesty? Or, a bold inference that if
push came to shove, the likes of O'Connor, Burke,
Shannon, could even pull a tune from the humble
container an instrument's carried in.

Tuning the instrument

The hand finds a tree...smooth bark, a knothole; ten paces
to the left...and here is a musical gate...four iron notes as
it opens. He inhales primrose; daffodils sound a welcome
as a winding ribbon of pathway leads up to the big house,
footsteps measuring out metre, the tongue lilting a fine
melody composed between watering holes, upbeat from
good succour! And now some hearty verses, foregoing
lamentation in favour of high praise for the new season,
a few lines dedicated to the hosts, only a bit of harmless
plámás to smooth reputation and appearance – hasn't he
dragged himself forwards through a rough hedge or two...

Feet on gravel, lift of the heavy door knocker – three strikes
for luck. Footsteps approach on the other side, a cough.
Final taste of morning air; a smile arranged, fond greeting
prepared: here is Raftery, strung, finely tuned, ready to play.

Touched

1979 –
punk rebellion
      inspired by simplicity
      songs with three chords
         jewellery made from safety pins

My own band, The Resisters
      made an album, toured
         Germany in an old ambulance
Berlin, Munich, Frankfurt –
      Eins zwei drei vier!

Back in London it was
      backs of lorries
         protest marches
      rock against racism, sexism,
         cruise missiles, army recruitment.

A heady time all round –
      improvised squats, dreams of turning society
         upside down – we were the future,
            beside and beyond ourselves.
               One, two, three, four!

Coda

Interdependence Day

When visitors from space arrive
and give us a fright, challenging
our right to manage the Earth –
we must show we are worthy
prove ourselves 'earthy'; drop
our weapons, hold one another
tight for all we're worth – show
we are worth it – how we can be
true to our souls, deliver those goals.
Sighting their impossible star-ship,
respond with partnership, joined-up
thinking and feeling, symbiosis not
psychosis; "all is interdependent," the
Dalai Lama says, so make amendment
change our ways, be just one part of
Nature alongside plants, animals, bugs
and bacteria; be like fungi mycelium,
entangled but not strangled by too
tight a grip; nurture more respectful
relationship with air, water, fire, soil –
without which we perish; cherish, put
an 's' back in front of oil – the number
of microorganisms in just one living,
loving spoonful is more than all human
beings that have ever lived. Return from
hubris to humus, forgo the pesticides –
agri-genocide, flinch at each plastic spoon,
cruel harpoon – say no more dead whales,
powdered rhino horns, pangolin scales ...
Show our visitors we understand the urgency,
that we'll emerge from this emergency with
competence and empathy – find inspiration
in Brigit, imbibe the flame of her spirit, affirm
how we are in this together; *together* – gather
and tether – show our true *meitheal*...

And when they say our time is up, even
as the credits roll on this planet B movie
rise from calamity, reclaim our humanity –
show we are sustainable, that we are able,
say "Hiya" to Gaia, re-soul – plant another
tree with Afri at Féile Bríde, a heart-seed
of hope and kindness – awareness along
with humility. Can we survive any other
way – it has to be *Inter*dependence Day.

Notes and Thanks

Thank you to Siobhan Hutson-Jeanotte and Jessie Lendennie at Salmon Poetry; to my partner and fellow writer, Moya Roddy for her close reading of the manuscript; to our daughter Cass for her creativity and inspiration; to Whitney Smith, Tony Curtis, Geraldine Mitchell and Adam Wyeth for their generosity in reading and responding to the poems; to Ted and Annie Deppe for poetry camaraderie and exchange; to all family and friends; to Oughterard Writers Group; to Galway County Council Arts Office; finally, to poetry editors and their journals and to the live venues that enable us to share our work.

The poem, 'Summer Time' borrows a line from Mary's Oliver's poem 'The fourth sign of the Zodiac, Part 3' – "Do you need a little darkness to get you going?" (Blue Horses, 2014).

'A Pangolin goes into a bar' echoes an article in the New Yorker by David Quammen (2020) 'Did Pangolin Trafficking Cause the Coronavirus Pandemic? The elusive animals' possible involvement in the origins of COVID-19 gives them a weird ambivalence: threatened and, perhaps, dangerous.'

'We are the Walrus' relates to the story of an Arctic walrus that turned up in Ireland in 2021, quickly acquiring the nickname 'Wally' and gathering a sizeable fan-base while continuing a roundabout tour of Wales, France and Spain, before eventually returning to its natural home in 2022.

In 'Thinking inside the box', the quote, "Everything seemed to be music to him", comes from singer, Seán Keane in a 2020 episode of the TG4 documentary series Sé Mo Laoch, featuring Mairtin O'Connor.

A short film of 'More!' with Grainne Malone and friends reading the poem was made by Roj Whelan: https://www.youtube.com/watch?v=PKs_xSCNIEM' 'Interdependence Day' was specially written for Féile Bride 2021, to mark the launch of the book, 'Interdependence Day: Teaching the Sustainable Development Goals through Drama for All Ages (Afri/Action from Ireland).

Acknowledgements

Versions of some of these poems have appeared, or are forthcoming in Abridged, Channel, The North, The Font, Scintilla, Journal of Wild Culture, Fusion Magazine, Berklee College of Music, Boston, USA; The Idler, Crannog, Ecological Citizen, The Avocet, Honest Ulsterman, Culture Matters, Reading the Future: New Writing from Ireland (Hodges & Figgis 150th Anniversary Anthology/Arlen House), Live Encounters, Orbis, Happy Birthday Mr Bob Anthology, Magma, Corvid Queen, Devour Art & Lit Canada: Panku Poems issue, Rhymerag, Dogs Singing Tribute Anthology (Salmon), Romance Options – Love Poems for Today (Dedalus Press) Just a Second – Exploring Global Issues through Drama & Theatre (Afri/Action from Ireland). 'Interdependence Day' was written specially for Afri's Féile Bríde Festival 2021.

A grateful thank you to Galway County Arts Office for awarding funding in 2020 towards writing and compiling this collection.

Comhairle Chontae na Gaillimhe
Galway County Council

PETE MULLINEAUX grew up in Bristol, UK – his first published poem, 'Harvest Festival', written aged 13, was included in a Macmillan anthology, *Poetry & Song*, and recorded on ARGO Records with music by Ewan McColl and Peggy Seeger. Living in London in the 1970-80s he was part of the original Apples and Snakes poetry collective and played with the left-wing punk band The Resisters, before going solo as Pete Zero. His anti-nuclear song 'Disposable Tissues' won the City of London Poetry/Song contest and was made into a single record, with proceeds going to the Greenham Common women's peace camp. Living in Galway, Ireland, since 1991, he teaches global issues in schools through drama and creative writing. His four previous collections are: *Zen Traffic Lights* (Lapwing 2005), *A Father's Day* (Salmon 2008), *Session* (Salmon 2011), and *How to Bake a Planet* (Salmon 2016). His work has been read and discussed on RTE's Arena and featured on the Poetry Programme podcast *Words Lightly Spoken*. He was selected for *Poetry Ireland Review*'s special 100th issue (edited by Paul Muldoon). A number of stageplays have been produced and three dramas for RTE radio. Two non-poetry books were published in 2021: *Interdependence Day – Teaching the Sustainable Development Goals through Drama for All Ages* (Afri/Action from Ireland) and a debut novel, *Jules and Rom – Sci-fi meets Shakespeare* (Matador UK).

PRAISE for *How to Bake a Planet* (Salmon 2016)

'*How to Bake a Planet* combines the sombre with the comedic…
(in) the singular voice of this poetry — one part sarcasm, one part
irony, two parts morbid bluntness — Mullineaux draws on
anxieties about a poisoned planet, strangled relationships, and the
ever-present ticking of time in an attempt to uncover the
smothered sentiments we all keep locked away.'

BRIANNE ALPHONSO — Jacket2 (USA)

'The journey is not without its moments of doubt and the
collection is peppered with a series of ecliptic moments
reminiscent of Edward Thomas's "stop at Adlestrop" railway
station, TS Eliot's "moment in and out of time" or Yeats's Irish
Airman's "in balance with this life, this death." All this adds up to
an intriguing and enriching collection of poetry, one that is
certainly worth several visits.'

DES KENNY — Galway Advertiser

'…the poems here are taut and possess a razor sharp wit…reminiscent
of John Clare…probing, beautifully written…a gem…'

JAKI McCARRICK — Poetry Ireland Review

'Each and every poem in *How to Bake A Planet* relates to the present
crisis…the agony of being part of the society that is mutilating
Nature…'

THRIVENI C MYSORE — Plumwood Mountain Journal (Australia)

'Mullineaux's strength lies in rallying a collective yearning for a
future in harmony with nature and extending beyond our own
individual bubbles… It curates a space where we can commune. It
makes us feel less alone.'

FLORRIE CRASS — Home-stage.com

PRAISE for *Session* (Salmon 2011)

'*Session* captures the wit, inventiveness, grace and connection of player to player, of musician to the natural landscape, of seasonal rituals to the deepest desires of the heart. This remarkable collection belongs in the library of every musician and poetry lover.'

Irish American Music & Dance Association (Minnesota, USA)

'With requisite craft he takes you into a world of observed moments, of habits and rituals, leaving you with a more enriched feeling of the occasion at hand...the power of now in poetic terms...a beautifully written work.'

Trad Connect (Ireland)

'*Session* is a beautiful magical book, soaked in waves of musical imagery and sound... written with impeccable craftsmanship, a delight on the ear and begs to be read out loud.'

The Ranting Beast (Ireland)

'Marvellous...these reflections and resonances are evocative and insightful. Mullineaux crafts genuine and perceptive surprises. More please.'

Orbis Magazine (UK)

'Mullineaux uses evocative images, insightful observation, humour, playfulness... He is a scrutiniser of intricacies, a watchful eye. *Session*, by Pete Mullineaux is a gem.'

Irish Music Magazine

'Absolutely exquisite...the poems could only have been written by someone inside the music.'

Celtic Connections Magazine (Denver, USA)

PRAISE for *A Father's Day* (Salmon 2008)

'Imaginative, innovative, intelligent and poetic...reminds me of the three Liverpool poets, Brian Patten and the others...a fine and beautiful book.'

PAT MCMAHON – Head of Galway/Mayo Library Services

'...gorgeous and resonant...with a stunning final blow.'

AILBHE DARCY – Stinging Fly Magazine, Dublin

'Mullineaux is a profoundly sensitive poet... while some lines are so grimly funny I'm genuinely jealous I didn't think of them first.'

KEVIN HIGGINS – *Galway Advertiser*

'...vivid verse that will take the reader on a roller coaster of emotions.'

Midwest Review (Oregon, USA)

'keen-eyed and lyrical...emotional and tender but also humorous, witty and philosophical, this is a brave collection from a wonderful poetic mind.'

GERARD HANBERRY

'Simple, luminous images...Mullineaux's voice carries lilts of John Cooper-Clarke. There are poems here to make one smile, frown, think; the comedian often gives way to a serious poet indeed. A fine book then, and beautifully produced.'

FRED JOHNSTON – Western Writers Centre

'These poems sing of deep humanity.'

GERALDINE MILLS

salmonpoetry

Cliffs of Moher, County Clare, Ireland

"Publishing the finest Irish and international literature."
Michael D. Higgins, President of Ireland